To Jean

KNICKERS

With best wishes

Rosemary
Hawthorne.
2008
xx

The friend of Fortune may you be,
May nothing bar her smile:
But, hand in hand with you, may she,
Show up in tip-top style!

S.K.Cowan.M.A.

The friend of Fortune may you be,
May nothing bar her smile:
But, hand in hand with you, may she,
Show up in tip-top style!

S.K.Cowan.M.A.

KNICKERS
An Intimate Re-appraisal

•

Rosemary Hawthorne

SOUVENIR PRESS

CONTENTS

This book is dedicated to my three daughters,
Samantha, Arabella and Phoebe.
Between them they know a lot about knickers.

Many of the items illustrated in the following
pages are taken from the author's collection.

PREFACE

When I first started to collect women's clothes I was more concerned with the outer than the inner coverings, but gradually I came to realise the importance of underclothes: if they are not in sympathy with the top layer the overall 'look' will not be right. Knickers were a late enthusiasm — but I have become more than moderately interested in this humble garment.

No other item of dress has suffered such mixed reactions — from pink-cheeked embarrassment to downright dirty-minded guffaws — or been subjected to so much ambiguous association. In satin and lace, it is the intimate gift of a lover; in botany yarn, the best hated part of school uniform; in snatches of lurex, a saucy token of promiscuity.

A bewildering variety of names has landed on it over the years: breeches, trousers, trowsers [sic], pantaloons, pantalettes, knickerbockers, knickers (knicks), small clothes, small wear (smalls), indescribables, unmentionables, inadmissables, bloomers, bockers, nether-garments, trolleys, divided skirts, step-ins, camiknickers, combinations (combs), pants, panties, pantees, briefs, scanties, passion-killers, French knickers, teddies, hi-kinis, tangas — and, the latest rhyming slang, Alans (Alan Whicker's). These, I suspect, are a mere drop in the ocean.

What follows is a social commentary, closely touching on women of every class.

ONE
PANTALOONING

The history of knickers covers barely two hundred years — nothing compared with that of other items of dress in the civilised world. During that time this article of clothing has seen many changes, but until the last decade of the eighteenth century our female ancestors cared not a jot about covering the lower part of their anatomy with a separate garment. Long skirts, a petticoat or two, corset and linen chemise worn against the skin were all the cladding felt necessary — or, indeed, healthy.

Contrary to present-day opinion, at that time the only women indelicate enough to wear drawers — a masculine garment — were said to be 'lewd, loose-moraled creatures of ill repute'. On such dubious foundations did knickers rise to assume the mantle of modesty.

In the 1790s the mood of fashion changed dramatically. In France the People's Revolution led to a simplification of all European dress: women wore high-waisted, Grecian-style draperies of soft muslin. The 'Empire' line was spectacularly sensual, elegant and fashionable — but very chilly. By about 1800, life for knickers had really begun.

❧   ❧   ❧

The first pair of knickers on the scene, called pantaloons, reached to below the knee or to the ankles and was made of a light stockinette in a

'flesh colour'. Reputedly it was worn by the lead-
ing ladies of the French Directory or 'dashers' of
western society who were in the front line of
fashion.

By 1820 nether garments were likely to be part
of the daily wear of duchesses, but it was to take a
good dose of Victorian propriety to urge the
disinclined masses into these newfangled articles.
Queen Victoria's reign (1837–1901) eventually
enveloped all but the poorest women in drifts of
chaste, white underclothes. Puritanically self-
righteous, clean and godly Victorians took
starched underlinen to a peak of sartorial excel-
lence. The French had only been playing at it; the
Victorians boldly structured the Great British
Knicker.

❧   ❧   ❧

The word 'pantalettes' (a diminutive form of
'pantaloons') is a nineteenth-century American
name for 'loose drawers with frills at the bottom
of each leg'. These were worn by children and
young women c1820–1850.

However, it appears that these novelties were
often imperfectly made, as a letter dated 1820
makes clear: 'They are the ugliest things I ever
saw; I will never put them on again. I dragged my
dress in the dirt for fear someone would spy them
. . . my first dimity pair with real Swiss lace is
quite useless to me for I lost one leg and did not
deem it proper to pick it up, and so walked off

leaving it in the street behind me . . . and the lace had cost six shillings a yard.

'I saw that mean Mrs Spring wearing it last week as a tucker. I told her that it was mine and showed her the mate, but she said she had hemmed it herself — the bold thing.

'I hope there will be a short wearing of these horrid pantalets [sic], they are too trying.'

The *World of Fashion*, an early nineteenth-century magazine dedicated to 'High Life, Fashionables, Fashion, Polite Literature, Operas and Theatres', was the *Vogue* of its day. Mrs Bell (married to the owner of the magazine and proprietress of a smart dress shop) was the wily fashion editor who dictated to society women exactly what they should wear — and then sold it to them. If Mrs Bell stated that ladies wore silk drawers on horseback — they obeyed and wore them, and under bathing dresses, too.

TWO
PIONEER DRAWERS AND BLOOMERISM

Nearly all mid-nineteenth-century underclothes are austere. You did not draw attention to the significance of what lay underneath, well wrapped, by a display of lavish needlework. Only the outer edge of the top petticoat, regularly glimpsed, was given a treatment of *broderie anglaise*. The rest was totally plain.

The fear of calling to mind anatomical facts was such that underthings were a taboo subject. As a Victorian lady aptly put it, 'these are not things, my dear, that we speak of; indeed we try not even to think of them.'

An upper- or middle-class woman wore a lot of clothes — even in summer. No sign of diaphanous muslin draped around the contours as in the 1790s. Now women were shrouded in yards of opaque material.

The first item that went on was the old-time chemise (shift, shimmy) which was like a wide sack, made of cotton or linen, reaching below the knees. Then came the 'divided' drawers, and the corset (proper name 'stays'). The camisole bodice went over the corset and she then stepped into the 'artificial hooped petticoat' or crinoline cage (invented by 1856) and several petticoats. Then she put on her dress.

So don't be surprised by the need for divided,

separate legs on her drawers. These were much easier for tackling the calls of nature 'out the back' or in the cold, Delft-tiled reaches of Thomas Crapper's up-to-date w.c.

Called drawers because they 'draw on' or 'draw up', the legs were attached individually to a deep waistband which fastened at the back. In the 1840s a certain Miss Pearson owned a pair which had wide tucks and were trimmed with knitted lace. They reached to mid-calf, were hand-sewn and fastened with a large linen button at the back — but had the added assurance of strong tape braces. So captivating were they, and so delectable Miss Pearson inside them, that they inspired an admirer to poetic flights.

MISS PEARSON'S PROPERTY

These drawers are plain
(Quite unlike thee . . .)
The needlework is fine;
Oh, Virgin Stuff, that has most right
To clasp those limbs sublime.
Would I could dolly, starch and iron —
Thus serve this pair divine —
For, dear Miss Pearson, I perceive
These longcloth legs are thine!

Victorian Washing Hints

Washing made easy: one of the best bleaching and emollient agents in washing person or clothing is borax. Dissolve in hot water, $^3/_4$ lb to the 10 gallons; a great saving in soap is effected by its use. It will not injure the most delicate fabric; laces and other fine tissues may be washed in a solution of borax with advantage to colour.

Washing, Ready and Effective mode of: dissolve 1lb of soap in 3 quarts of boiling water, the night before washing. Beginning to wash, put the soap into the dolly tub, add 8 tablespoonfuls of spirit of turpentine, and 6 ditto of hartshorn. Pour upon the above 8 gallons of boiling water. Have the clothes ready assorted; begin with the fine ones. Dolly each lot about five minutes, wash them in hot water in another dolly-tub, if you have it, next in blue water. When the water is getting cool, put it into the boiler to boil kitchen towels and other greasy things.

N.B. The quicker the washing is done, the better. As soon as one lot is taken out of the dolly-tub put another one in whilst the others are being rinsed. A little pipe-clay dissolved in the water employed in washing linen cleans the dirtiest linen entirely, with about one half the labour, and saving full one half of soap. Blueing: The blue bag is used for white articles. It helps to make them a better colour, and prevents them from going yellow. A few drops of ammonia added to the blue water helps to make them even whiter.

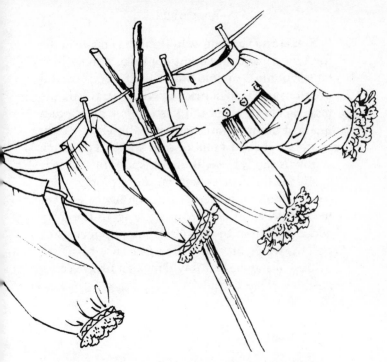

Lace: white lace should be washed with white soap in fairly hot water. Change the water frequently, and add soap to all as lace does not need rinsing. Pin to dry on a board covered with linen cloth. Fine lace is never ironed. To colour lace after washing, put into warm water to which sufficient made coffee has been added to colour the lace (straining the coffee first through double muslin). Honiton lace should be folded evenly together and tacked lightly in a piece of flannel. Double the flannel over it and squeeze constantly. Never use hot water. Pull into position and leave to dry down. Do not iron.

Starching: boiling water starch is made in the following way: one tablespoonful of starch, three tablespoonfuls of cold water, half a teaspoonful of borax and a small piece of white wax. Mix the ingredients to a smooth paste, pour on about a quart of boiling water, stirring all the time until smooth, and add a pint of cold water. The starch is now ready for use. If one teaspoonful of sugar is added, the articles will be more glossy when ironed and retain their stiffness longer. To prevent starched artcles from sticking to the iron, add a little alum to the starch before pouring the boiling water on. To stiffen lace, use cornflour instead of starch, as this will make it firm, yet not stiff; never starch fine lace.

❧   ❧   ❧

Various White Materials Associated With Victorian Underclothing

FLAX: The plant *Linum usitatissimum*, bearing blue flowers which are succeeded by pods containing linseed. It is cultivated for its textile fibre.

LINEN: Cloth woven from flax.

COTTON: The white fibrous substance which cases the seeds of the cotton plants. Thread spun from cotton yarn. Any fabric made from cotton.

CAMBRIC: (1530). A kind of fine white linen originally made in Cambrai, in Flanders.

BATISTE: (1697). The original name of the Cambrai-born maker of cambric.

LAWN: Named after the French town of Laon, an important place for linen manufacture. A fine linen cloth resembling cambric.

MUSLIN: (1609). From the town of Mosul in Iraq, where this delicately woven cotton was first made.

MULL: A fine cotton muslin originally made on the island of Mull, Scotland.

NAINSOOK: (1804). Urdu/Hindi — *nain* meaning 'eye', *sook* (or *souk*) meaning 'pleasure'. A fine cotton fabric.

JACONET: (1769). From Jagannathpuri in Cuttack, a town in India; a cotton fabric originally made there. Lighter than shirting.

POPLIN: (1710). Dubiously held to be the feminine of 'papal', so named because originally made at Avignon, a papal town from 1309 until 1791. A woven fabric, silk warp, worsted weft, that has a corded surface. Now chiefly made in Ireland — imitation wool or linen material.

CALICO: (1540). Also called *calcut*, from the name of the Indian city. Cotton cloth originally imported from the East. English production (1578) — a plain white cotton cloth that is coarser than muslin.

LONG CLOTH: (1545). A cotton or calico made in long pieces.

❦   ❦   ❦

L. O. Acres.
No. 4: 1851.

Professional seamstresses made up underclothes for middle- and upper-class women, usually in sets of a dozen. In the mid-nineteenth-century they would have earned about one shilling (5p) a pair.

I have a pair of ankle-length drawers from this period, completely divided, tying round the waist with tapes (or strings as they were called). They are hand-sewn — the white cotton poplin exceedingly neatly hemmed with tiny stitches. The date, marked on the waistband in Indian ink, is 1851, the year of the Great Exhibition at the Crystal Palace. The owner's name and set number are also marked.

Many women continued to wear these 'long legs' up to and beyond the close of the century. You may imagine the heart-stopping sight they must have been for men, seeing them dart, artful as mice, from beneath volum- inous skirts. At a shilling a pair they were cheap at the price. Men, of course, had known the discreet luxury of wearing underpants for

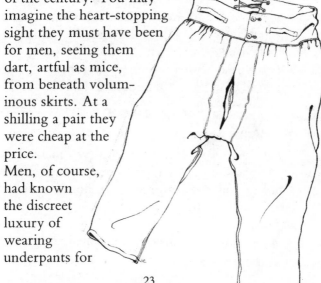

hundreds of years before women caught hold of the idea. An early Christian martyr, St Pantaleone, has been immortalised for posterity by giving his name, via a series of complicated changes, to the seat of modern life — in short, pants.

The Italian Renaissance of the sixteenth century used a comic character in their plays, an old, feeble-minded man who wore very tight-fitting trousers as part of his costume. 'Pantalone' became a stock character still seen as part of modern circus acts or in pantomime. Just to confuse you more, in the eighteenth and nineteenth centuries, men's underpants were called drawers and, originally, women's drawers were cut on very masculine lines.

Lady Chesterfield, writing to her daughter around 1850, commented: '... skirts that ended one inch above my ankles showing the vandyked or frilled edges of those comfortable garments which we have borrowed from the other sex, and which all of us wear but none of us talk about ...'

❦   ❦   ❦

The mid-nineteenth century started the great debate on Dress Reform. The ever increasing width of the skirts (dangerous with open fires and candles) and the continuing fashion for tight-laced corsets (malformed bodies, misplaced organs, stillborn babies) brought medical opinion and some private individuals to public attention.

The most captivating and memorable of these has to be Amelia Jenks Bloomer. Mrs Bloomer, a governess, married her Quaker husband, Dexter, in 1840 and went to live in Seneca Falls, New York State. She was an inspired woman for 'the cause' and her first great project, as an officer of the Ladies' Temperance Society, was the 'Demon Drink'. Defeating this social evil was her duty to family life and she was appointed editor of the society's newspaper, *The Lily*, in 1849.

Mrs Bloomer became concerned with other aspects of women's lives, including what they wore. Ironically, it was a friend of hers, Libby Miller, who designed the practical dress 'fit for any sort of locomotion' that Mrs Bloomer, in 1851, was to make so famous. In essence this was a moderately full skirt that reached a little below

the knees and, beneath it, baggy Turkish style trousers that strapped at the ankles. This Mrs Bloomer wore, extolling its virtues to her readers. Many disapproved of the liberated dress, but other women copied Mrs B's example and Bloomerism took to the streets. She spoke at rallies all over the United States on topics relating to Women's Rights and Healthier Dressing; many people laughed and jeered when they saw her. But she was a brave, convinced woman, forty or fifty years ahead of her time.

❦   ❦   ❦

Whilst there was much concern in the minds of gently-born people in the early part of the nineteenth century over the seemliness of grown women wearing nether garments — they conveyed an image of masculinity and admitted the sensual presence of legs — they had no such misgivings when it came to their children. Up to the age of five years, it was thought perfectly correct for boys and girls to be dressed in almost identical clothes, right down to the drawers or 'trousers'. These were allowed a good 'peep' of leg-ends under their skirts. Young girls continued to wear this style until the age of thirteen.

Marchpane, a wax-headed doll of the 1840s, was handsomely dressed in hand-sewn clothes that were specially made for her. She had the lot — dress, petticoats, chemise, corset and her 'shams', cotton 'legs only' tied to her sawdust-

filled thighs. Poorer-
class children in the
early nineteenth
century often wore
false drawers,
trousers or
'pantalettes'
like these.

A crinoline cage of the 1860s would have been jolly draughty for winter wear and a substantial pair of drawers would have been needed to protect the nether regions. Thick flannel and heavyweight woollen material were the answer, like the robust pair of open-legged drawers which were made for a rotund lady (39 inches / 99 cms around the waist). They were in a very thick material, fleecy on the inside, called angola. Reputed to have been made for a French princess, they must have been of great comfort during inclement weather in the early 1860s.

🐾 🐾 🐾

In 1851 a new invention was patented by Isaac Merrit Singer — the sewing machine. Clothes could now be made far quicker, but the early simplicity was lost beneath a welter of trimmings.

A pair of blue striped, Welsh flannel drawers, very homely articles indeed, combined hand-stitching with some machining. Small pieces of material had been inserted to give extra width at the back, and the leg ends were bound with coarse blue blanket stitches. They were made between 1875 and 1880.

By the 1870s the crinoline had ceased to be fashionable and the bustle took over. Figure-hugging bodices with tight waists swept smoothly over accentuated hips into the generous, pillioned folds of the skirt. The front of the skirt narrowed considerably, all the interest being concentrated at the back. These exaggerated swags of material were caught inside by tie-tapes.

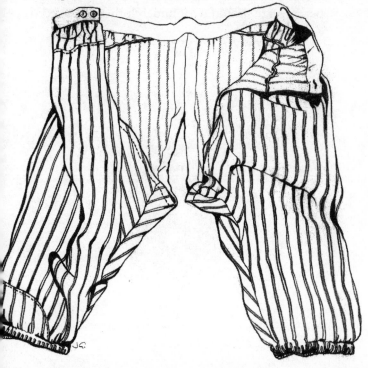

The first Women's Suffrage Committee was formed in 1866, and by the 1870s many women supported it. Not only 'The Vote' but simple things like physical education in girls' schools were campaigned for. In the 1880s there was a tremendous 'health' cult and a renewed cry for simpler dressing for women. In 1881 Viscountess Harberton led a group of convinced society women into forming the Rational Dress Society (shades of Mrs Bloomer) and the following year a 'Hygienic Wearing Apparel' Exhibition was held at Kensington Town Hall. Lady Harberton wrote: 'No growing girl or woman of child-bearing age should wear underclothes that exceed 7 lbs in weight.'

One of the pioneers in this health movement was Dr Gustave Jaeger, MD, Professor of Zoology and Physiology at the University of Stuttgart. In the 1870s, while some manufacturers were advocating chamois leather underclothes for 'everyday wear', he was busy writing his first essays on health culture which were eventually published in 1878. Dr Jaeger's Sanitary Woollen System inspired the cult of woollen underwear, not only in Germany, but in Europe.

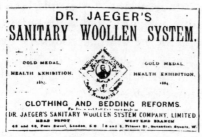

Jaeger passionately believed that pure animal fibres would prevent or cure every ill by 'preventing the retention of noxious exhalations of the body'. An early convert to the 'woollener' movement was an Englishman, Lewis Tomalin, who secured the sole rights to the Jaeger name, system, patents and trademarks, gave up his grocery business and, with two cousins, started to manufacture the natural, undyed woollen underclothes for men and women, from small premises in Fore Street, London. In 1884 he won a gold medal at 'The Healtheries', an international health exhibition, and earned praise from the medical profession for the beneficent properties of Jaeger's Woollen Underwear. After this the carriages flocked to Fore Street and the famous 'Jaeger's' was well and truly launched.

After Jaeger's sanitised invention there came a whole range of similar underwear, and there was also a trend towards brighter colours. From the time skirts began to expand in the late 1840s to 1860s and needed the support of the crinoline cage (or masses of petticoats), drawers had taken on a new significance. There was a burst of colourful 'underneaths' — purple, scarlet and even tartan were considered 'quite charming' for drawers and the 'new' knickerbockers. Scarlet — a hot favourite in the 1880s — earned itself a music hall song, entitled 'The Red Flannel Drawers Grandmother Wore'.

A pair of home-made red flannel open-legged drawers has survived from 1880–1890. Machine-stitched and hand-sewn, fastening with two buttons at the back, they reached to mid-calf and are fretted with large moth holes (moths seem to appreciate red flannel!). These drawers, altered on several occasions, must have caused quite a stir beneath the starched white petticoats.

THREE
KNICKERBOCKER'S GLORY

The American writer Washington Irving created a fictitious character, Diedrick Knickerbocker, whom he used as a *nom de plume* for his book, published in 1809, called *History of New York*. 'Herr Knickerbocker' is described as a descendent from the original Dutch settlers in the New Netherlands of America and is thus a 'New' Yorker.

The illustrations for the book were done by the humorous artist, Cruikshank, and he depicted the 'Family Knickerbocker' menfolk dressed in loose breeches, tied or strapped at the knee in the traditional Dutch way.

Knickerbockers caught the popular fancy and gradually became part of the wardrobe for middle- and upper-class men for wearing on 'sporting occasions'. By the 1860s some shrewd women had taken to wearing the same sort of garment under their huge crinoline skirts when engaged in such active pursuits as 'gardening, brisk walking or rock climbing'.

❦   ❦   ❦

Misadventures

From Lord Cowley's *Memoirs*, 1855:
    'Despatch from our Ambassador in Paris on the visit of King Victor Emmanuel. Lord Cowdrey

reports that at a state reception a Lady in Waiting had the misfortune to trip over her crinoline skirt and tumble headlong in view of the Imperial party, whereupon the King exclaimed with enthusiasm to the Empress, "I am delighted to see, Madam, that your ladies do not wear *les calecons*, and that the Gates of Paradise are always open!"'

From a letter written by the Honourable Eleanor Stanley, Lady in Waiting to Queen Victoria, in 1859:

'I hear that the last new "fast" ladies' fashion is said to be wearing "knickerbockers"'; and she describes how the Duchess of Manchester, climbing too hastily over a stile during a paper chase, 'caught a hoop of her cage in it and went regularly head over heels, lighting on her feet with her cage and whole petticoats remaining above her head. They say that there was never such a thing to be seen — and the other ladies hardly knew whether to be thankful or not that a part of her underclothing consisted in a pair of scarlet tartan knickerbockers which were revealed to the view of all the world in general and the Duc de Malokoff in particular.' The latter's comment afterwards, *'Ma chère, c'était diabolique!'* seems fairly apt.

❦   ❦   ❦

The diminutive form of knickerbockers, 'knickers', became commonplace by the late 1870s. In

KNICKERS

the female fashion jargon of the late nineteenth
century 'knickers' alluded to a closed gusset
undergarment, albeit pinched from the male
wardrobe, that at first, risked the wearer's repu-
tation as a 'lady'. Such theft, initially considered
fast, became fashionable and, finally, common.

Such is the power of the word that even now,
when it has been around for well over a hundred
years, 'knickers' — if said in unprepared company — still has quite an effect.

A superb pair of knickers, amply cut, very
finely hand-sewn in best quality cambric with
closely worked pin-tucks and white embroidered
vandyked frills at the leg ends, was put by as part
of an elaborate wedding trousseau for a bride in
1885. The knickers fastened with the new-style
side-placket buttoning but still had 'strings' to
pull tightly round the waist. The owner's initials
were embroidered on the front of the garment,
and they have survived as a most handsome
example of Victorian knickers, a traditional
'bottom drawer' piece of underclothing.

Most of the clothes that form museum and
private collections come from the wealthier sec-
tion of the population. These people had the
money to buy lots of clothes and the room to
store them. Poor, working class people of the
nineteenth and twentieth centuries relied on the
secondhand clothes markets, hand-me-downs or
pickings from the rag-men's hoards. In a desti-
tute family underclothes were non-existent or, at
best, very patched and worn.

THURBERS
SNOWFLAKE
PASTRY FLOUR
5 lbs. nett.

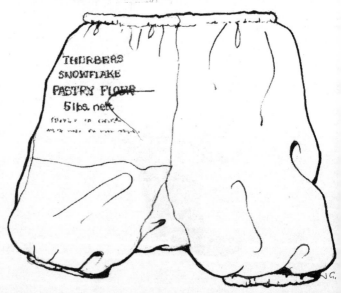

For a wife and mother who could use her needle and who taught her daughters to sew, a good source of material could be found by utilising the cotton sacks in which grocers stored large quantities of flour, rice or sugar. These sacks were boiled white and then used to make underclothes. The practice continued up to the Second World War.

There were drawbacks. Small boys used to yell 'Rice Bags' at women in the street, but the most humiliating aspect was the way the indelible trade and weight marks often refused to boil off completely. Pity girls (and boys) who had to put up with '28 lbs Aerated Pastry Flour' brandished on their backsides.

❧ ❧ ❧

Nothing pleased the higher orders of Victorian society more than having their name on something or, if possible, everything. They dearly loved marking ink and used it constantly. The better managed the household, the more ink. Underclothes needed identification with the owner's name or initials, because in a large household there were a lot going through the laundry. This was either part of the house or the responsibility of a local laundress to collect, wash, starch, iron and return.

Names were often embroidered onto the 'best' underlinen. A girl approaching marriageable age, preparing her trousseau, would sometimes have two lots of initials — her maiden, then later her married name added. If there was a cypher or a family coat-of-arms, so much the better.

J. & J. Cash Ltd. of Coventry had originally been ribbon weavers and mercers, but with the depression of the ribbon trade that began in 1860 they turned to making cotton frilling for under-clothes and pillow-slips and all manner of in-sertions and embroidered edgings. In 1889 they had the idea of manufacturing personal woven name-tapes which could be ordered at the haber-

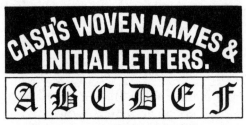

FOR SEWING ON HOUSEHOLD LINEN, SOCKS, AND UNDERCLOTHING.

Any Name can be had in any Type for 6s. 6d. a Gross.

The Letters are manufactured in Three Sizes of Old English Type in Turkey Red. Orders can also be executed in Black, both of which are warranted per-fectly fast. The price of the Single Letters in Red is 2s. 3s. and 5s. 6d. per gross box.

SHIRT LABELS manufactured in every variety. Samples and Prices forwarded on application.

J. & J. CASH, Coventry.
SOLD BY DRAPERS AND HOSIERS EVERYWHERE

dashery counters of drapers' shops. Those same name-tapes are often a vivid reminder of school-days — onwards. Shops such as Frederick Gorringe in the Buckingham Palace Road used to offer customers who purchased school uniform or trousseau linen from them the additional service of sewing on the name tapes.

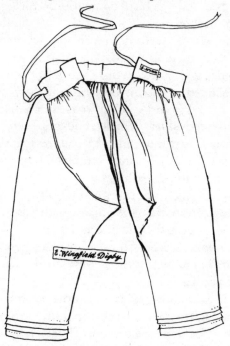

A pair of 1860s hand-sewn cotton drawers in my possession bears a Cash's name-tape which must have been added nearly 30 years later at least — proof of the lasting quality that was expected from Victorian underclothes.

Young women of the 1890s sped forth, un-
impeded by outraged elders, fashionably attired
in their knickerbocker suits. These were the gen-
eration of New Women, perched precariously on
their 'safety' bicycles, pedalling furiously
towards the twentieth century. Better education
for women, a stronger voice in a man's world,
the beginnings of birth control — all these helped
them on their way.

Publicly as well as in private, women now
admitted to being bipeds: the floating swans had
gained legs. Newly discovered independence
was echoed in the introduction of the bicycling
dress, a jacket and knickerbockers or a discreetly
cut divided skirt. Knickerbockers were called
'Rational Costume' since Viscountess Harberton
and her friends in the Rational Dress Society
patronised this stylish garb.

Tweed knickerbockers and woolly pantaloons
did not mean that the jolly Boadiceas weren't
happy to wear frilly knickers when the occasion
demanded. Indeed, some of the prettiest, most
entrancing underclothes come from the 1890s
and early 1900s.

It is fascinating that the more women took
control of their own lives, the more provocative
and sexy became their undies. Typical drawers of
this period were hand-sewn in fine cotton, with
strings at the waist, deep insertions and frills of
handmade lace. 'Squared', recessed leg ends were
a popular detail of the time. They were alluring,
coquettish, decidedly candidates for the term

'lingerie' as against prosaic 'underclothes'.

Throughout the nineteenth century and up to the First World War the vulgar term for divided drawers was 'free-traders'.

❦   ❦   ❦

The humble maidservant of the 1890s was likely to be found in serviceable dark blue striped cotton, machined knickerbockers, Often both knees would have large patches over the holes that had been worn when she turned up her skirts to scrub the floors. There would be a complicated fastening at the back — a placket or flap of material, secured by three enormous bone buttons. This was called the 'trap door'.

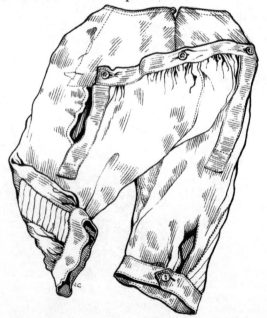

An actress, presumably a bicyclist as well, sang this delightfully shocking verse in the 1890s:

> Just a little bit of string — such a tiny little
>   thing,
> Not as tightly tied as string should be;
> So in future when I ride, I shall wear things
>   that divide,
> Or things that haven't strings, you see!

Would this lady have passed a cycling proficiency test?

There was also a popular Victorian couplet relating to the celebrated Charlotte Collins, the London-born Music Hall star who made famous the song 'Ta-Ra-Ra-Boom-De-Ay':

Lottie Collins lost her drawers
Will you kindly lend her yours?

In the 1890s Lottie Collins would perform a frenzied, abandoned dance to accompany her song. My grandmother recalled that this ditty was the result of a mishap one evening during Miss Collins' act.

❦   ❦   ❦

Despite the growing assertiveness among women and the ribaldry about knickers in the theatre, in some quarters old-fashioned prudery still held sway. In large department stores and drapers' shops, the underwear and lingerie counters were always discreetly tucked away upstairs where there was less danger of male trespassers chancing on these reticent delights, and in magazines and advertisements illustrations of drawers and knickers often depicted the garment demurely folded, leg to leg, leaving much to the imagination but less to concern the sensibilities.

❦ ❦ ❦

Horrocks were cotton manufacturers who diversified into the ready-made linen and underwear industry in the 1860s. The invention of the sewing machine had given them the ability to make clothes as well as just provide other manufacturers with material for garment making.

In trade catalogues of 1867 they are named 'Horrocks's guaranteed well-made, ladies machine-sewn calico underclothes', and very early they achieved the distinction of a brand name. A pair of calico knickers from about 1900, with back-flap fastening, buttons and strings, is marked with a Horrocks's label. The price, written in pencil, is 4/11d (approx. 25p).

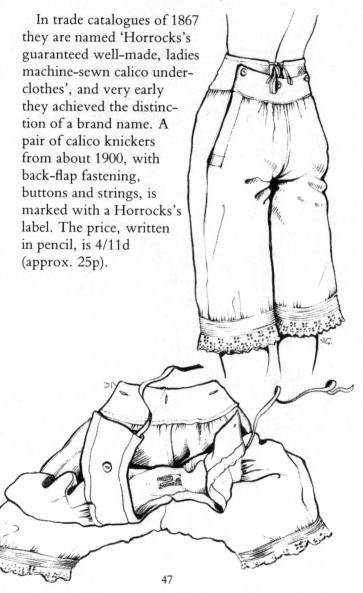

A true-life example of 'how to get on in society' was the devastatingly pretty Ethel who came to London to be an artist's model, but felt her name too dull for such a career and changed it for the more inspiring one of Amaryllis. She never looked back. She was a great success and in due course met one of the painter's clients, fell in love, married 'well to do' and lived happily ever after. Her hand-sewn, lace-trimmed drawers, dating from about 1900, have the name 'Ryllis' discreetly embroidered in a garland of flowers on the back.

FOUR

COMBINATIONS —
A BLESSED UNION

In 1901 Queen Victoria died and her elderly,
self-indulgent son, Edward VII, came to the
throne. During his nine-year reign women
dressed in some of the most beautiful clothes ever
to tempt the daughters of Eve. It was no secret
that the King loved and admired feminine
beauty: the Court and High Society echoed this
royal partiality and favoured women who were
elegant and well groomed. Lace, high-necked,
full-bosomed blouses, tiny waists, long trailing
skirts trembling with cascades of frills like the
wash of a ship — all these featured in fashionable
dress of the early 1900s.

The flowing, 'cello-shaped bust and hips
demanded sleeker underclothes and combinations became very popular. These had been
introduced during the 1870s, a happy marriage
between the chemise and drawers. The corset
was worn over the top of them.

Some could be very pretty indeed, like the pair
made as part of a wedding trousseau in 1901.
Reputed to have been made at a convent, they
were of excellent quality, the fine mull muslin
sewn with a profusion of tiny pintucks and lace
insertions. The garment fastened down the front
with small linen buttons, and the open legs ended
in very wide lace flounces. In deference to the

year of National Mourning for the old Queen, the bride had black ribbon threaded at the neck and legs.

Lingerie Modes

Ready-made white underwear may now be bought so cheaply that some perhaps marvel at our presuming to offer designs at all. But we venture to think that there are many amongst our readers who are still of opinion that quality is better than quantity; for, despite the show in the shop windows, we are really very much where we were thirty years ago.

The design we give in sketch No. 59 is beautifully planned, the under-arm pieces cut in one with the front, and the upper part

of the back arranged with a seam down the centre, and on to this the full back is set in neat gathers. A single, long dash shapes either front, and on the right side a false hem is laid and stitched either side for the accommodation of the buttonholes.

The top takes a graceful V shape, and is inlaid and edged with Valenciennes. A deep frill of cambric outlined with lace forms the sleeve, while a similar frill, treated with insertion and edging like the top, finishes the knickers at the knee.

From *Home Chat*, 1895. The design was called 'Camilla', and the price of the pattern was 6$\frac{1}{2}$d (approx. 2$\frac{1}{2}$p). It could also be supplied tacked up for 1s 6$\frac{1}{2}$d (approx. 7$\frac{1}{2}$p).

❧ ❧ ❧

Aertex was invented over a hundred years ago. It was the idea of a Monmouthshire MP, Mr Lewis Haslam, and two medical men, Sir Benjamin Ward Richardson and Dr Richard Green. They had been discussing the benefits of wearing wool, particularly when it was new, fluffy and therefore airy — advantages that were soon lost in the weekly wash-tub. Mr Haslam was a great believer in fresh air: not only should it be breathed, but it should allow the skin natural insulation against heat and cold.

The gentlemen decided that a material was wanted that could 'hold' air although repeatedly worn and washed. Cotton was the obvious choice — it was a matter of finding a weave that would provide the air-pocket structure. Haslam set up the Aertex Company in 1888. At first they manufactured only the revolutionary new material with holes in it, which was sold on to clothing manufacturers, but it was such a success that in 1889 larger premises were needed and Aertex started making their own garments for men. By 1891 women's underclothes were in production and the company continued to expand to meet the world-wide demands for their products.

A pair of Aertex combinations of 1900 is well cut and neatly tailored to fit the waist. Seven linen

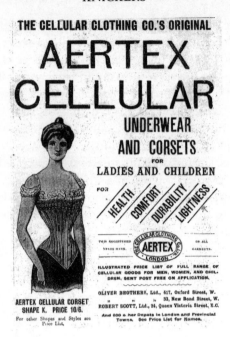

THE CELLULAR CLOTHING CO.'S ORIGINAL

AERTEX CELLULAR

UNDERWEAR AND CORSETS

FOR

LADIES AND CHILDREN

FOR

HEALTH COMFORT DURABILITY LIGHTNESS

AERTEX LONDON

ILLUSTRATED PRICE LIST OF FULL RANGE OF CELLULAR GOODS FOR MEN, WOMEN, AND CHILDREN, SENT POST FREE ON APPLICATION.

OLIVER BROTHERS, Ltd., 417, Oxford Street, W.
"   "   33, New Bond Street, W.
ROBERT SCOTT, Ltd., 26, Queen Victoria Street, E.C.
And 600 other Depots in London and Provincial Towns. See Price List for Names.

AERTEX CELLULAR CORSET
SHAPE K. PRICE 10/6.
For other Shapes and Styles see Price List.

buttons form the front fastening with a small lace trim at the neck and sleeves. Measuring 42 inches (107cms) to the knees, the original red and black label reads: The Cellular Clothing Company Ltd. Aertex London. Quality 987.

❧   ❧   ❧

Another brand-name combination garment was made from extremely fine woollen locknit. This almost transparent yarn was called 'Merino' and loomed from the best quality sheep's wool Australia could export. It was as soft as cashmere and most durable.

I have a pair of these combinations dating from 1910. They are front fastening with mother o'pearl buttons. Although close-fitting over the body, the breasts are given a bit of room by the simple device of inserting 'lemon'-shaped gussets — remembering that the corset was still worn over the combination. They are 42 inches (107cms) long.

The original machined label at the back has perished, but on the right side of the garment is stamped, in indelible blue ink, the manufacturer's logo: 'The Rameses Registered Unshrinkable. Made in England'.

The best of both worlds could be yours, as this article in *The Lady's Magazine* of 1901 explains:

> With the summer before us, we shall be thinking of light woollen underwear, believing, no doubt, that nothing else is safe in this changeable climate of ours. I wonder if anyone will follow my advice, and try Dr. Lahmann's cotton-wool underclothing! It is prepared on the most scientific principles. People find it absolutely comfortable, and when wearing it they are protected from chill; and having once taken to it, they never return to the all-wool underclothing, which is constantly irritating to the skin, and is ruined by washing. Dr. Lahmann's cotton-wool underclothing can be had in every weight, from the thinnest to the thickest.

❦   ❦   ❦

FIVE

SILK, SIN AND ELASTIC

Edward VII died in May 1910, and the fashionable world trembled at the first tremors of significant change; it had been good to be rich and in royal favour. The years of frou-frou skirts rustling, unrepentant and seductive over silk petticoats, were about to end.

Heralding the momentous transitional period, women's outer clothes became classically slender. By 1911 skirts 'hobbled' at the ankles had become fashion's fancy. This ridiculous, impractical style was indulged in by only a few fashion extremists. Stride for stride, 'hobblers' could not keep up with ardent Suffragettes. A hobble skirt when women were on the brink of loosing their historical chains? Functional tailor-mades and sensible underpinnings were what was needed.

Silk had been the natural choice for only the very rich or aristocratic. Consequently there was not a great demand for silk underclothes and most of that was

57

not made until the late nineteenth century or during the Edwardian period. Silk undies spawned a sort of inverted snobbery; as one elderly lady remarked, 'Silk was thought to be only available to the nobility . . . or actresses. My mother considered no well-brought up, middle class girl in the early 1900s should wish to wear silk underclothes.'

LADIES
FLEECED KNICKERS

The gently-reared, upper class woman of 1909, however, would clothe herself in open-legged drawers of the finest *crêpe de Chine*, professionally hand-sewn and finished with a deep frill of handmade lace and silk bows. The height of decadence it might have been, but the daring Lucy Wallace, sister of the equally notorious novelist Elinor Glyn (she of the 'sin on a tiger skin' fame), yielded her first talents as a dress designer to making luxurious silk lingerie for rich, famous and aristocratic women. Society thought these underclothes 'simply ravishing' and Lucy — in private life Lady Duff Gordon — and her 'Maison Lucile' became an instant success.

Contrast between fabrics and trimmings is a feature of most clothes in the early years of the twentieth century. Fine silk or wool edged with bold braids, raised embroidery or chunky lace are common mixtures.

Irish crochet lace was a particular favourite. This is a complex, solid, often three-dimensional form of crochet worked in heavy linen thread with a very fine hook. An irregular arrangement of 'bars' links various parts of the design — this is called 'guipure'. Flowers and leaves are the usual motifs found on this strong lace. In my collection I have an extremely elegant pair of transparent lawn drawers with a two-button back fastening. Hand-sewn, with embroidered initials and

trimmed with deep 'cuffs' of Irish crochet lace, there are two bespoke loops sewn to each side of the drawers to hold the ribbon bows in place. They were made in about 1910.

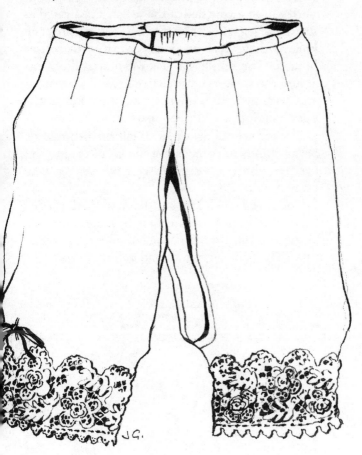

JG.

Schoolgirls in 1913 wore drab, grey/brown twilled cotton school knickers as part of their uniform. Still referred to as 'rationals', they were worn under a heavy pleated 'drill' slip (gym slip) with a long girdle tied at the waist. Elasticated at waist and leg ends (they reached to just below the knees), they were originally worn with cotton linings. The emphasis was on practicality, enabling the wearer to move from reading, writing and arithmetic to a smart game of hockey without changing any clothes apart from footwear.

But the schoolgirl of 1913 had the promise of better things to come: soon she would enjoy the prettier, abbreviated underwear of the post-war years.

The first French knickers have to be those delicious frillies that mesmerised the male audiences at the Moulin Rouge in the late nineteenth century. The swirling white underclothes erotically

contrasted with the black silk stockings and scarlet flounces worn by the 'Can-Can' dancers.

Petticoat drawers — or divided skirts — were an early twentieth-century version of contemporary French knickers. A pair made and worn in France about 1914–15 have button fastening at each side of the waist and very, very full legs attached to a slender hip yoke. They are professionally made, machined and hand-stitched and have a Swiss embroidered edging. These knickers were designed to double as a petticoat under the wider, shorter skirts that were becoming fashionable.

Romantic Diversions

The 1914–18 war inevitably brought heightened romance. Some sentimental wives and girlfriends embroidered their undies with regimental badges — but pretty motifs were more usual, such as butterflies, an ancient Chinese symbol of happiness. Two butterflies seen together are a mark of married bliss. This design was obviously popular and is often found embroidered on trousseau undies, even today. On a pair of knickers made around 1915 the insect, exquisitely embroidered, appears four times, on back and front of each leg. It is clear that this bride wished to make doubly certain.

Another pair of First World War knickers has the name 'MAUDE' writ large and then embroidered on the front waistband.

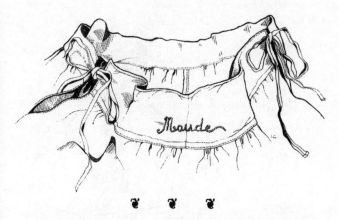

❦   ❦   ❦

Grace Good has kept a pair of child's knickers which she made at school in 1914 — when all girls were taught to sew as a skill for life. They are a triumph of needlework, the stitches small, neat

and varied. The wide bowed shape of the knicker is attractive. The school 'Open Day' label is still tacked into place, for these knickers, like all perfect samples, were for looking at, not using.

I received a letter from a woman who described the sort of knickers she wore as a child in 1914. She was the youngest of five children born to a working class family and her mother was a dressmaker. Mother made all their clothes, including the underclothes. The woman had worn simple 'trap door', back opening, calico combinations with a very short buttoned fastening at the front neck. These, she said, were quite a struggle to get into and out of! However, she had cause, at the age of six, to thank her mother for her clever design when she was approached by a man with obvious evil intentions. She managed to escape, unharmed, because of the complicated construction of her 'combs'.

❦ ❦ ❦

The First World War is a rich vein of research for the costume and social historian alike. The changes that took place during those four years mark the start of the truly 'modern' woman. As the classes of society slid imperceptibly into different structures, fashion, like so much else, simplified. The clothes became easier to wear; whaleboned corsets were chucked away and, with them, many Victorian-held attitudes.

Wider, more flexible ideals went with uncomplicated dressing.

The 'envelope chemise' was the first shot at what we call a camiknicker. Dresses were fairly straight and shapeless — therefore the undies had to match. Uncluttered lines were perfect for easier sewing and certainly quicker to make.

ENVELOPE CHEMISE.
Pattern No. 5954.
Sizes small, medium and large.
The medium size requires 2¼ yards
of 36-inch material.

The old-fashioned chemise played out its last role in 1915. A small strap of material, three-buttoned, linked the crutch. Given the long and dignified history of the chemise, 'how are the mighty fallen'.

❦ ❦ ❦

I don't believe it . . .

The following appeared in *The Lady* in November 1915:

The Modesty Combination. This ideal garment is a perfect production, affording the maximum amount of warmth with the minimum of bulk, the attached skirts woven into shape by an expert process.

. . . surely no one need be that modest?

On the other hand, at the same time more up-to-date underwear was also being designed. A pattern for simply structured French-style knickers, cut in a 'pilch' shape, was printed in *Girl's Own Annual* in 1915. 'Pilch' is a seventeenth-century word meaning a triangular flannel wrapper worn over an infant's diaper or nappy.

ଏ ଏ ଏ

Ping!

We only think about elastic when it goes slack and doesn't do the job it's intended to do — namely, hold things up or pull things in. So how did it start and what did they do without it?

In the eighteenth and early nineteenth centuries they used small spirals or springs of brass wire to 'elasticate' things like garters. (Try holding your knickers up with brass springs . . .)

By 1820 elastic webbing had been invented by a Mr T. Hancock of Middlesex. This wasn't elastic as we know it, nice stretchy stuff, but cloth treated with a solution of Indian rubber (caoutchouc) which dried in fibres. By the 1830s this was occasionally being used for corsetry, but it became sticky, smelly and perished very quickly.

It was Charles Goodyear, of motor car tyre fame, who in 1836 discovered a way to make the gum stable.

Elastic, the sort of thing we buy now, wasn't manufactured until the First World War. Having undergone hundreds of tests in the clothing industry, it certainly did not become boil-proof until after 1925, when the Dunlop Rubber Company became the biggest Anglo-American concern to develop natural rubber elastic and, eventually, synthetics.

During the early part of the twentieth century, troops returning to Britain after serving in the Indian Campaigns under Lord Seymour brought home, as souvenirs for their womenfolk, transparently thin Indian silk gauze drawers. These garments were nicknamed 'See Mores'.

Dancing to Freedom

The most popular dance of the First World War was the Tango. The craze had started in 1909 when this exotic, thrilling dance swept across the dance floors of Europe and America. From the smart hotels in Biarritz and Boston to the tea-rooms in Bournemouth, every girl wanted to tango. It was a dance that called for agility, lissom stride and non-restrictive clothes.

Paper patterns were printed with instructions on how to 'run up' a pair of tango knickers,

which would allow for easy, unhampered movement on the well-waxed floors. A pair made in
1916, of black sarsenet (a fine, soft silk), are
roomy, with elasticated waist and legs edged
with three frills of black silk lace. Altogether they
are somewhat daring — like the dance.

Combinations during the First
World War reflected this new
freedom — made of cambric,
machined and hand-sewn with
a lot of embroidery and insertion lace. They were shorter in
length, reaching from waist to
knee, with very wide legs.

73

When jazz music moved from New Orleans to Chicago and St Louis (in about 1917) it started the great dance cult that was to grow in popularity throughout the 1920s and '30s. Evening clothes were tremendously influenced by this black American music — and so were the undies. I have a charming pair of *crêpe de Chine* knickers, hand-sewn with lace trimmed, high cut leg-ends and elasticated waist. They have hand-embroidered motifs of a piccaninny looking at a jack-in-the-box, and date from about 1918.

SIX

BRIGHT YOUNG THINGS AND OLD DIRECTOIRE

After the 1914–18 War underclothes were smaller, lighter, and the chaste white of former decades, practical but emotionally neutral, began to retreat in favour of colour. Better dyeing processes meant that lingerie materials could be all the colours of the rainbow. Top of the list was 'peach' — it was back to the 'flesh' tones of the French Directory period.

By the mid-1920s the skirts had shortened to the knee and the new figure was 'boyish'. No bosom, no bottom, no curves at all were required. The flappers twirled long beads, powdered in public, rouged their knees and kicked up their heels in the Charleston, revealing the minimum of underwear.

A pair of camiknickers (camisole and knicker combined), made by a woman undergraduate at Cambridge in 1925, were peach-coloured charmeuse (a soft, fluid satin), hand-sewn with lace trim and three buttons to fasten at the crotch. She recalls how daring she felt to wear such a liberated garment. Yellow voile (semi-transparent cotton) camiknickers are also found, with fairy-like vandyked hem and small ribbon ties between the legs, and a pair of pale pink satin French knickers, made between 1928 and 1930, have cream lace appliqué on the sides. The Harrods label states that the garment is pure silk and made in France.

Perhaps the prettiest pair of camiknickers I have seen is in transparent pale blue georgette (a filmy silk crêpe), with bodice top edged with heavy needlepoint lace. They were handworked by the present owner's sister in 1927.

❧   ❧   ❧

The old open drawers were not worn much after
1920 — the arrival of the short skirts put paid to
them — but there is a delightful story of a nurse
and doctor examining an old lady during the late
1930s. When asked jokingly by the nurse why she
continued to wear these old-fashioned articles,

she replied, with some asperity, 'I like to air me parts!'

There is no answer to that...

'Directoire' is a word used to describe closed gusset knickers that are elasticated top and bottom. It is a memorable name. It was revived from the late eighteenth century: those 'Directoire' ladies or 'dashers' had worn pantaloons or

This Dainty Camisole is so pretty, with its ribbon-threaded waist lace, and the Directoire Knickers are delightful wear.

breeches of a similar style in 1794–99, the French Directory period. A pair of cream *crêpe de Chine* directoire knickers of about 1920 had wide bands of satin and *ecru* lace inserted on the side seams. They were professionally hand-sewn.

One of my favourite items in the collection is a camibocker (camisole/with bocker bottom) which is made in cream 'washing' silk, with the back of the cami and 'trap door' fastened with seven large mother o' pearl buttons. It was made in the bespoke lingerie department of Debenham and Freebody in 1929. Many large stores encouraged their customers to order undies that could

be made up in the workrooms to special designs.

A woman 'turning out' came across a romantic possession that had been tucked away for many moons — a pair of French knickers which she had worn on her honeymoon in 1925. They are exquisite in every detail, made from cream-coloured net with chiffon appliquéed in an abstract design, oversewn and edged with cream silk. The front and back have heart-shaped satin centre panels. These pretty knickers are entirely hand-sewn, with side-button fastenings, and were made in Hong Kong. Extremely delicate sewing like this reaffirms how skilled the Chinese are at decorative work.

French knickers such as these — semi-trans-

parent and bewitchingly seductive — sometimes called 'Mother trusts me' knickers.

❦   ❦   ❦

HOTEL DE PARIS
MONTE·CARLO

9th August 1931

Dearest Daphne,

Everything is bliss! The weather, the place, the hotel — Everything!

Most bliss is Reggie. He is too heavenly. This is the luckiest girl in the world!

What a relief it's all over! I couldn't bear another happy day like that in a lifetime.

Love and kisses,

Prue.

P.S. Reggie, the darling, has just bought me the most divine undies you ever saw. Ravissant! Daphs, the knicks are unbelievable..... positively indecent!! I'll never dare wear them in Esher.

Prue's 'unbelievables' consisted of two pleated panels of peach-coloured satin with a hinge of silk connecting back and front at the waist. They were based on an early Egyptian (1400 BC) loincloth called a *schenti*.

81

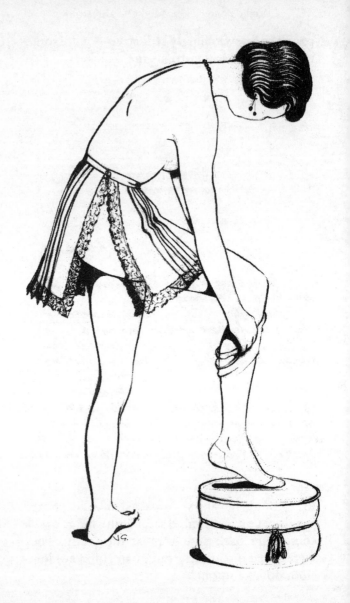

In the late 1920s and '30s great fashion influence was exerted by the 'silver screen'. Hollywood sought to take over the fashion crown of Paris and women aspired to look like their favourite film actresses. On and off the studio sets, famous film stars aroused enormous public interest in what they wore.

The technique used to make the stars look slim, elegant and sexy was bias-cutting. Cutting across the weave of the material had previously been little used by designers, but now the figure was revealed in an entirely new way: softly feminine with natural curves. Women became exceedingly figure-conscious, and dieting and 'health and beauty' exercise were very popular. And as the outer clothes became closer-fitting, the underwear did too — only more so.

As the Duchess of Windsor, formerly Mrs Wallis Simpson, is reputed to have said, 'You cannot be too thin, nor too rich.'

Camiknickers, nowadays sometimes called by the American name of a 'teddy' ('an all-in-one that loves to hug you'), remained fashionable and so did French knickers which were now often bias-cut and combined machining and hand-sewing. A pair in my collection, in lemon silk, is decorated with ribbonwork and has scalloped edges trimmed with lace.

From about 1920 the French-style knickers were called 'step-ins' by Americans.

For wearing beneath fitted ski-clothes or riding jodhpurs the 1930s woman had fine silk

stockinette breeches (pantaloons). I have a pair
marked with the label Elliot of Hawick Scotch
Underwear.

Man-made textiles were an idea thought up a long time ago. In 1664, Robert Hooke, an English scientist, suggested that artificial threads could possibly be spun from a 'glutinous substance' following the example of silkworms. A French scientist during the eighteenth century put forward the theory (correct, as it happened) that gums or resins, drawn out in fibres, would produce a yarn from which an artificial material might be made. His name was René de Reaumur. But it was not until 1905 that 'rayon', the later trade name, first went into production. In 1910, two hundred and fifty years after its initial concept, artificial silk, 'art' silk, was commercially produced and used by the American Viscose Company to make soft-collared shirts.

Between the First and Second World Wars it successfully provided ordinary women with the

material they sought to make clothes. Rayon looked and felt like luxury silk, it was ideal for undies, and it was cheap to buy. At last there was a substitute for silk.

I have two pairs of rayon directoire knickers of the 1920s and early 1930s. Safely gathered in at the knee with a double band of elastic, one pair is white and very, very shiny (sitting on a chair must have been difficult!); the other is blush pink and has a deep, pointed waist yoke and a floral appliqué made in the dull reverse of the material.

In the face of such fierce look-alike competition, the real silk lingerie manufacturers had to persuade women that what they offered was still the best. A 1931 *Home Chat* advertisement is blatantly patronising, smugly suggesting that silk knickers are not only what you really want, but are better, purer *and cheaper* than their artificial counterparts.

Home dress-making is a domestic skill not as prevalent nowadays as it once was. Thrifty and nimble-fingered women of the 1920s and '30s could indulge in every aspect of this absorbing occupation. There were many easy-to-understand patterns and cheaper materials available to make lots of clothes, including undies. Artificial silk was advertised under a variety of names: Courtauld's Ltd stated that their brand 'Delysia' had a 'texture like rich *crêpe de Chine*, but priced for economy'.

Weldons Ltd, a fashion, patterns and transfers publisher, produced illustrated journals aimed at women in the home, living on a tight budget. Their monthly Transfer Series of the 1930s had 'Slim Fitting Undies' on offer. There were dozens of different styles, plus a free pattern and sheet of embroidery transfers included in the 6d (2¹/₂p) price.

23132
Chemise and Directoire Knickers.

Women's magazines laid particular emphasis on the home-sewer using her talents to make presents: 'Don't forget, dainty home-made undies are a useful and most acceptable gift.'

SEVEN

PARACHUTES AND PASSION KILLERS

The years of the Second World War brought restrictions and regulations to civilian life. 'Make-Do and Mend', Austerity, 'Utility', these words form a sombre backdrop for fashion during those frightening years.

Inevitably, with material in short supply, the fashion industry underwent a period of stagnation. Garment manufacturers were asked to take on other work more seriously concerned with the War Effort. Women, however, are always wonderful during a crisis. With imagination — and a touch of creative humour — they managed to get by even when beset by the most stringent clothes rationing.

Handknits came into their own. Women unpicked their old woollens and made up new. It was a popular, portable pastime — your knitting went everywhere from the kitchen to the air-raid shelter. All kinds of garments were knitted — including knickers and camiknickers, and I have pairs of both, made from 1940s 'Stitchcraft' patterns. Home sewing also thrived. Out of necessity clothes were unpicked, turned round and re-made in different styles. The only way to have feminine undies was to make them yourself.

A woman showed me the pair of black cotton textile lace camiknickers which she had made in

1945. As she said, 'It was the end of the War; you couldn't buy anything pretty — and I hadn't seen my husband for several years.'

No more need be said; the home fires were still burning.

Knitting in War-Time

Is Both National Service and a soothing Black-out Hobby

From the *Daily Express* War Time Needlework booklet.

The trademark of the War years is the significant 'Utility' label found attached to all manufactured clothing from 1942, through the post-war years, up to 1953. To catch sight of it on a piece of clothing is to have immediate contact with 'rationing'. These were years of wearisome, economic pressure. Everyone was hard-pushed to make the 'coupons' last out, particularly if there was a growing family.

Three coupons had to be surrendered to buy a pair of knickers.

The CC41 (Clothing Control 1941) became a very famous symbol. Its designer was Reginald Shipp. He lived in Barnes, London, and in the

late 1930s worked as a commercial artist for an old-established firm, Hargreaves, whose premises were near Oxford Street. Hargreaves were designers and suppliers of manufacturers' labels; their work covered retail, clothing, club and uniform labels. In 1940 Hargreaves, amongst several other companies, were asked to submit designs for the Utility mark that the Board of Trade wished to issue in 1941. Reginald Shipp's design was selected and he received, along with his company, a letter of commendation. The Board of Trade also awarded Mr Shipp a personal prize of £5. Reginald Shipp died in 1962 and the firm of Hargreaves is no longer in existence.

Shipp's mark is surely one of the great, classic designs of the twentieth century. It is as famous as fish and chips and, certainly, as British. Sadly, like the originator of that famous repast, the creater is virtually unknown — yet thousands of people instantly recognise his work as being a well-remembered part of their daily lives.

❦   ❦   ❦

Black lace has been around since the sixteenth century. The French town, Chantilly, began producing fine silk lace in the eighteenth century and became renowned for its black lace in the 1870s, but it was not until the early twentieth century that black lace, handmade or machined, became the essential ingredient of seductive underwear.

Once its power had been discovered, the western world was pleased to take every romantic

advantage. The old black magic really does work! I have a pair of black silk machined lace French knickers, the waistband and legs trimmed with electric blue satin. They were made around 1940 and once belonged to a chorus girl who I was told 'entertained the troops'.

❧   ❧   ❧

Nylon was patented and in production just before the outbreak of the War. After eleven years of research by the American company, Du Pont, this entirely synthetic fibre was first used commercially in 1938 to make stockings. But, almost immediately, production was restricted to the War Effort and nylon was used to produce rope, tents, parachutes and many other vital supplies. Occasionally, a consignment of damaged parachutes was released from military into civilian hands. These might be made of silk (particularly good quality from the First World War) or, later, nylon. What treasure trove this was if you could sew! The large triangular strips that formed the 'chute made up into excellent underwear and, if necessary, a wedding dress. Many a bride walked down the aisle in the latter years of the Second War wearing a bit of a parachute.

There were disadvantages — the nylon was dense and meltingly hot to wear.

A pair of French knickers was made in 1944 as part of a wedding trousseau. Superbly hand-sewn, with stitching so precise that it looks like machine stitch, they were made from nylon para-

chute pieces. They have a side button fastening
and are edged with old Buckinghamshire lace.

❦   ❦   ❦

Women in the Armed Services during the Second
World War were issued with directoire knickers
in drear uniform colours — khaki, navy, black,

blue/grey. The directoire style was considered necessary under the regulation knee-length skirts of 1941.

These unflattering knickers were dubbed 'passion killers' and the name is now part of the nostalgic annals of war. They do, however, seem to have gathered a few other emotive names over the years: 'ETBs' (elastic top and bottoms), 'boy bafflers', 'wrist catchers' and the obscure 'taxi cheaters', are among the best known.

I have a number of these over-elasticated, baffling, wrist-catching, cab-cheating, emotional murderers in my collection, including a pair of black knickers of about 1945 made in 'Celanese' (trade name of the British Celanese Company Ltd.), an artificial, locknit material, and a pair from about 1940 in pale pink rayon, with machine-embroidered forget-me-nots.

There is also a pair in lobster-pink 'slipper' acetate satin, machined and very neatly hand stitched — the sort of hideous garment I was still being taught to make at school in the 1950s.

An ex-Wren told me that their dark navy or black issue knickers were called 'black-outs'. They were absolutely loathed and generally never worn. Kept only for uniform display at 'kitmuster' inspections, the only time she remembered wearing them was for the annual medical check when it was a 'knickers only under dressing gown' order.

❧ ❧ ❧

Evacuating Ellie

Ellie was rising three when she was evacuated from Camberwell Green, South East London, to the depths of a Dorset village. Besides her label and gas-mask, she had a little suitcase of belongings — a few dresses, woollies, vests, socks, a 'Liberty' bodice and some knickers. All were simple, handmade, often cut-downs, patched and well worn.

I don't know what became of little Ellie, but a few years ago I was given her case of clothes which had remained, by some miracle, untouched in the village. It is a very rare bundle indeed. People usually only keep 'posh' or better clothes, the rest gets thrown away, so this small wardrobe of Ellie's provides an important record of what a poorer class child would have worn between 1939 and 1945.

Ellie had frocks and knickers to match. This was commonly the way infant girls were dressed, in every class, from the First War to about the mid-1950s. There are floral cottons for summer and wool for colder days.

One outfit is made of coarse grey mohair tweed — obviously cut from a woman's dress. The frock and wide bloomers that go with it must have been hatefully itchy for a small child to wear, even allowing for the protection of the 'Liberty' bodice.

❧   ❧   ❧

A woman who was at school in the late 1920s revealed that she wore 'large knickers made of denim which were thick and hot, with elastic so tight I thought I would be permanently scarred, under which were worn white liners, equally hot. We changed the blue ones every three weeks and the white liners once a week...'

Like the deeply felt complaint voiced above, I too, as a schoolgirl of the early 1950s, echo a strong fellow feeling. My school knickers were fleecy-lined, bottle-green yarn, with a pocket. Cotton linings were always worn. The greatest discomfort was the heat, for they were terrifically hot to wear. They were also ugly and unfeminine.

I must record that as far as I can tell there were no sad songs sung over the passing of these vile coverings.

However, as a dress historian researching knickers, I was forced to admit that I did require one or two pairs to look at. But, try as I might, I could not unearth a single pair of the ghastly things. I concluded they had all met with a terrible end — burnt, buried or reduced to rags. Imagine my surprise when, having almost given up hope, I was sent a whole boxful, neatly packaged and catalogued, and found that my generous donor was a man.

I can never thank him enough. He supplied, in navy-blue, bottle-green, maroon, scarlet, grey and brown, the missing links in this story. If nothing else, these school bloomers have character — and most impressive labels. From the 1930s, 1940s and 1950s they read like the symbols

of respectability they are: MONTFORT,
WOOLLATON, ALPINE INTERLOCK,
BAIRNSWEAR, QUALESTA, CHILPRUFE,
COSICURA and the splendid PURITEX
HYGIENIC — surely Headmistress Approved!

Ah, is all forgot?

EIGHT
WEAR TODAY —
TRASH TOMORROW

Christian Dior, the French fashion designer, launched his famous 'New Look' in 1947. He re-created a pleasingly curved, cinch-waisted woman who wore post-Edwardian-style clothes, long full skirts and frothy underwear. She was in stark contrast to the short-skirted, square-shouldered, sensibly tweeded and hand-knitted creature who had been coping with a war.

The nylon patent was granted to the British Nylon Spinners in 1939 and Bri-nylon became a famous trade name in the late 1940s and '50s.

A selection of 1950's nylon knickers and briefs.

St Michael
Nylon Lingerie

Knickers were designed in the French style, though younger women favoured 'briefs'. They were manufactured in plain and printed nylon and acetate materials — often trimmed with nylon frills or lace. The high street clothes shops were full of drip-dry, easy-care underwear.

A 'disposable' society was about to take shape.

❦   ❦   ❦

Gussie Moran, a handsome, blonde American girl, took Wimbledon by storm in the summer of 1949. It was the result of some stylish tennis — she reached the Ladies' Doubles final — and of her eye-catching panties.

'Gorgeous Gussie' as she was affectionately nick-named, made a season of pedigree lawn tennis really hot stuff by wearing a pair of frilly lace panties, designed by Teddy Tinling. These were meant to be seen by spectators and news journalists alike.

When the All England Croquet and Lawn Tennis Club was formed in 1877, the lady members played polite garden tennis and wore, as they did for the first Ladies' Championship in 1884, long white flannel skirts, tight belts, petticoats, corsets, bustles, straw hats and, certainly, well-hidden drawers.

Suzanne Lenglen was thought shocking in 1920 when she appeared in a simple pleated knee-length dress with firmly gartered white stockings. Helen Jacobs was the first woman to wear shorts at Wimbledon in the mid-1950s. Gussie slammed tasteful Wimbledon in the eye and brought sex to the Centre Court — and, if we're honest, is remembered more for her knickers than her tennis.

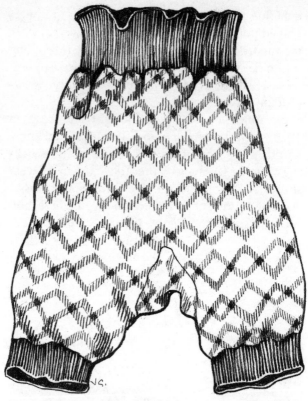

The 1960s rapidly increased the range of nylon polyester textiles. Women's outer clothes became fashionably short — the mini skirt was at its briefest in the late 1960s — and many clothes were decidedly functional. Trousers and jeans were, as now, consistently unisex.

Undies had to be sleek and figure-hugging: 'bikini' pants were very popular in stretch nylon yarn. Colours were hot and strong patterns favoured: lime, pink, purple, orange all blazed together. Many women still preferred traditional white or pastel underclothes, but the important thing was they had a choice.

Since everything had to be machine-washable, polyester, Banlon and Lycra were the materials men and women sought. Paper panties were manufactured in 1969, but after an initial success their appeal had waned by the mid-1970s.

It is hard to find examples of ordinary high street fashion underwear from the past 40 years. Nylon has made us a wasteful, throwaway society. Knickers were — are — continually replaced; they don't even make it to jumble sales. Secondhand knickers aren't 'nice', so, unlike their Victorian counterparts, not destined to retire quietly amid lavender and mothballs. The rubbish tip is the place for them.

❧   ❧   ❧

The only knickers to survive as heirlooms are likely to be the expensive designer makes — we hold dear what we pay a lot for — and in this 'exclusive' world Janet Reger is queen. She was talented and enterprising enough to design and market for the luxury trade in the early 1970s. By re-creating the silk and lace romance of the early twentieth century, Miss Reger provided her High Society — or merely rich — customers with the revived charms of seductive, feminine underclothes.

She has had many imitators since, but, like 'Lucile' before her, she revealed the right mood of underwear at exactly the right moment.

In 1964 Barbara Hulanicki, another designer, started a small mail-order business based on a pastiche image of sultry Hollywood vamps. Her

designs were imaginative: sexy emphasis on Art Nouveau, in dark sludgy colours and fluid materials. Very soon she opened 'Biba', a boutique in Kensington where the fashion-conscious young came to browse and buy in the dim, Tiffany lamp-lit shop. Hulanicki opened a further, larger store — but after a meteoric blaze of fame Biba's success fizzled and it was forced to close in the early 1970s. I have a pair of Biba camiknickers in terracotta-coloured 100 per cent cotton jersey, trimmed with lace in the same colour, dating from around 1970.

❦ ❦ ❦

From the vampish to the vulgar! My collection includes some red, white and blue stretch nylon souvenir panties that were worn to a 'bad taste' party on Royal Wedding Night, July 29th, 1981.

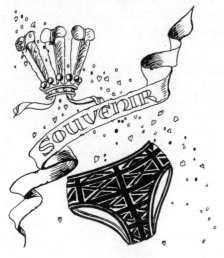

A Siberian wind blows across our shores — and our thoughts turn to warm-as-toast undies. Ladies' woollen underclothes have been made by firms like Wolsey, Morley, Chilprufe and John Smedley's for almost a century. Thermal is the modern fabric which keeps Jack Frost from nipping the nether parts. It is a manufacturing process whereby air is trapped in small cells or pockets — thus holding the body's own heat between the material and the skin. It is exactly the same principle that founded 'Aertex' in the 1880s.

'Damart', an underwear mail-order company, specialise in winter warmers and have developed thermolactyl, a mixture of synthetic and natural fibres. Wolsey still do a large percentage of their products in pure wool and, for luxury, cashmere.

Woolly combinations are rarely worn now, but Marks and Spencer and other large companies have fashionably feminised long johns within their popular ranges.

Tag End

Do you look at the label to see who makes the knickers and what they are made from? It's often surprising that what looks just like silk isn't, and what seems to be pure cotton has got something else in it as well.

Labels are fascinating, a mine of interesting information. My daughter recently bought me a pair of bright, cherry-red velvet bikini briefs for my collection. They are made by a French company, Huit. They look like velvet, they feel like velvet — but, by heck, no way are they velvet. The tags tell me they are: 77 per cent acetate, 15 per cent polyamide and 8 per cent elasthanne — unless you happen to be wearing them in the United States, when they are suddenly 77 per cent acetate, 15 per cent nylon and 8 per cent spandex.

A rose by some other name . . .

NINE
NEXT TO NOTHING

I was once told by the owner of a 'naughty knicker' shop that the thrill-a-minute provocative bits of nonsense that create the illusion of wanton lustfulness are often purchased by men — and, just as often, returned by the woman in question and exchanged for something more robust!

The G-String

This is a single thin string, often decorated, attached to an elastic strip round the waist. It was originally the basis of the stripper's wardrobe — but now it has deviated into certain High Street shops, or mail-order catalogues.

Of these, Frederick's of Hollywood stands as the classic. This American mail-order company, under the zany direction of their 'in house' designer, Mr Frederick, has been in the daring underwear business since 1946. The catalogue has a wide range of fun-filled pages promoting G-strings with pockets, boost-you-up bras, fanny shapers,

hippie helpers and teeny-weeny split crotch biki-
nis. All the outrageous products are described in a
suitable breezy, risqué manner.

Like saucy seaside post-card humour — seen to
be fun.

❦   ❦   ❦

Just for the record; a Californian company successfully markets the 'Incredible Edible Candy-
pants' in a 'Wild Cherry Flavour'.

Now, that really does take the biscuit.

❦   ❦   ❦

In 1984, the designer Calvin Klein made it fairly
plain that, in this liberated society, men and
women could share the knickers. He designed a
range of knickers for men 'with women in mind'.
What our Victorian forebears would have
thought I shudder to think . . .

Innovative creative design flourishes in every
area of fashion — including knickers. Season
after season designers, manufacturers, advertising and marketing teams need to lure customers
into tenderly set traps.

It's not called underwear any more, nor lingerie, nor undies. Now 'intimate apparel' is the
contemporary phrase. Expensive advertising
campaigns often promote an image of romantic
luxury . . . and why not? Or maybe you are after
something more practical and prosaic? None of
us can hope to need poetic, alluring pants every
day of the week. Without doubt, that kind will be
in the shops, too. There is something to suit

every purse or pocket, every feminine mood and, goodness knows, that is almost limitless.

Among the latest designs is an enchanting pair of French knickers. Very finely pleated polyester in black, with a repeated pattern of shaded roses in pink and white, it is made by Charnos plc and called 'Degas', part of this company's 1991

'French Impressionists' range. Charnos, originally hosiery manufacturers, were founded in 1936. They commenced lingerie production in 1958 and have since diversified into other areas of garment making, including corsetry, knitwear and sportswear.

Or what about a crazy pair of minimal, white polyamide knickers — complete with rolling plastic eyes and fluffy red nose — also made in 1991?

Finally, 'Red hat, no knickers' goes the old saying . . . and it may be right at that.

TEN
INTIMATE RE-APPRAISAL

Sixteen years is a long time in fashion. Red hats have been given the shove; now it's 'fur coat, no knickers'. Such is life.

Since coming out and exposing my knickers to print in 1991, I've been sent most interesting letters, often enclosed with a knicker or two. These garments, some more enticing than others, tumbled through the Vicarage letterbox, eager to tell their story. Warmly, I thank those kind, generous souls who provided grist for my mill. My husband has now retired and we live in an anonymous house – but stray knickers still arrive at the door seeking refuge. So, here are a few of these lately-come-by knickers – the lavender ladies, nostalgic aunts', larky uncles', and (in an effort to keep up with Posh and co.), a couple of hot-off-the-shelves High Street chicks.

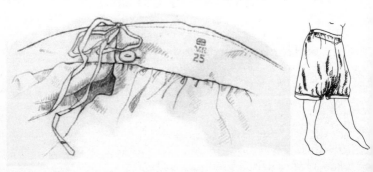

I had long-craved a pair of Queen Victoria's drawers to give the collection gravitas, so I was delighted when (after a little delay – the letter went to the wrong vicarage) a splendid pair of voluminous Queen Vic's arrived. The waistband measures a noble 48 and half inches and bears the V.R. cipher. Dignified? Yes. Romantic? No. Severe and totally un-amusing, they are old-fashioned 'splits' with a button-over back flap and pin-tucked leg-ends. Made from the finest linen, they are sewn superbly; I marvel at the painstaking work gone into making these dreary drawers. They are 1850s in style, but were probably made in the 1880s.

I assure you that drawers weren't all plain and no-nonsense in Victorian times. A dazzling, pretty pair of 1890s' drawers was sent by a family with royal connections; unfolding these charmers from their tissue paper, I discovered exquisite soft pink silk, with fine lace insertion, and caught with satin bows.

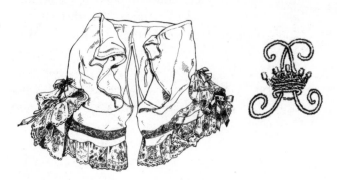

They are delicious, naughty, how-the-other-half-lived lingerie. I am fairly certain they were made in the workrooms of 'Lucile' the Society designer I mentioned in Chapter 5. Lucile called her seductive lingerie 'Sensations'; believe me, they are.

Do you remember Felix the Cat? I was sent a marvellous, rare pair of knickers, made for a child in about 1940. The elastic is slack, the fabric faded (with big holes), but they are printed with clear images of Felix the Cat.

Created by animator Otto Messmer, Felix first appeared in 1917 at the American film studio of Pat Sullivan, who specialized in cartoon features. After Felix's film career ended in the 1920s (the 'talkies' killed the cat), he continued to be a popular comic-book character for children. Was this pair of bloomers made out of old curtains during the War? Did the owner have a dress to match? I bet she did.

The nice thing about collecting old knickers is occasionally finding a forthcoming man. I did a show with my knickers at Bishop's Stortford and, for levity, included some men's underpants. I mentioned that, because dull compared with ladies' knickers, most gents' pants eventually get binned or used as dusters. While I was signing books after the show, a gentleman told me he had some 1960s pants he would send. A few days later, a package arrived containing a cereal box – with two, pristine briefs inside. One was a pair of Aertex  Supermesh 'Y' fronts ('Pull to shape when wet'), the other, the Holy Grail of underpants – string. 'Y' fronts have been around since the 1930s, and 'string' ones from the 1950s, but examples are scarce so this pair of Brynje ('The Original Norwegian String Underwear') filled me with joy. Bless you, Richard.

Tit and bum has always attracted a following in London's Soho. When Vivienne Westwood's son, Joseph Corre, and the designer, Serena Rees, founded 'Agent Provocateur' in Broadwick Street, they had a good chance of success. The tiny, deluxe lingerie shop opened in 1994, tempting women and their men to buy the naughty, somewhat pricey, but pleasing underwear that 'didn't need to squeak or whistle'.

Now Agent Provocateur boutiques have sprouted everywhere. They fill the gap that shops such as

Agent Provocateur

dear 'Rose Lewis' of Knightsbridge (see Chapter 11 of my book 'Bras') left behind. Agent Provocateur lingerie is witty and seductive. Their mailorder and online catalogue make it easy to buy. Whatever your age, dears, it is fun to get a pretty box, tied with ribbon, containing sexy underwear, especially on a wet Wednesday when you're doing the housework!

The one I chose for the collection is 'Kitty'; a blue silk, black ribbon side-tie bikini, with a printed motif of black lace and 'Agent Provocateur' written with a flourish across the backside.

But there are sad knickers, too.

When Diana, Princess of Wales died in 1997, like millions of others, I recall the shock and disbelief on hearing the awful news that brought so much sorrow. Clothes to symbolize mourning have a long history. Victorian mourners, not shy of death, were constantly prepared to present themselves in bombazine and crape at the first hint of a 'passing', court or cottage.

In the late 20th century things had changed. Apart from the sombre blackness of the Queen, family and close friends, there appeared to be little in the way of 'national' mourning clothes. Maybe it was not on show. A Knightsbridge friend of mine purchased a pair of knickers during 'The Great Grief' that she later gave to the collection. They are white cotton, black-edged briefs, with 'Harrods' embroidered in black across the side. These are important panties historically, since this fine shop will be forever linked with Diana's tragic death.

Some knickers become stars. When Helen Fielding wrote *Bridget Jones' Diary* in 1996, a film followed with Renee Zellweger and Hugh Grant in 2001. When at last the diet obsessed, chain-smoking, wine-swigging singleton, Bridget, gets down to intimacy with her man, he discovers her 'extra control'

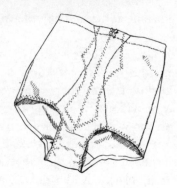

knickers. 'Hello there, Mummy!' he exclaims, and with that, Big Knickers were IN.

Control pants have been around since before the 1960s when they took over gradually from roll-ons and grim girdles. These days they are light and comfy to wear. Recently, I bought a pair of 'Bridget's' for the collection. I chose Camille, size 22, in 'Nude' (my Mother would have said 'beige'), with a double-strength, double-stitched panel across the tummy. They are 80 per cent polyamide/nylon and 20 per cent Elastane. Girdles, by another name, are creeping back.

The next pair of knickers are 'magic'; a word much used since *Harry Potter* arrived. Tiny, Hobbit-sized, tan-coloured 'Lycra' knickers, they stretch and redeposit flesh to present a flat front and a pert behind, and squash the rest into submission. Various types of magic knickers abound; 'Spanx' is a well-known name, and they are Trinny and Susannah's secret weapon. The 'Magic Slimshort' I spied for sale at a Ladies' Luncheon is known as 'shapewear'. This one came in a plastic pot with a screw top lid (possibly to keep them fresh). A 'Fanny Shaper' is what cheeky Mr. Frederick would have called them in the post-war Hollywood glamour days. Mind you, a lady brought me an old pair she'd found when cleaning out a sports' pavilion. They were in a bad way. Slack and baggy, tired and worn – the magic had vanished.

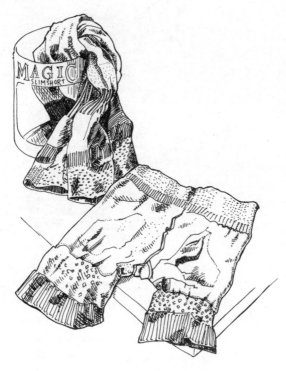

Big occasion, fun-loving knickers keep popping up. Perhaps you celebrated the New Millenium wearing mini cotton briefs with a silver starburst and 'Year 2000' exploding across your tum, courtesy of Marks & Spencer? Or were you a loyal football fan and wore New Look's glittering 'I Shop For England' girl boxers, complete with "06" and red and white ribbons. Were they binned afterwards?

Whatever, there is definitely more jolly sex seen on the High Street these days. At one time shops like 'Ann Summers' had blacked-out windows and catered for 'sleazy, raincoat-brigade' blokes. But the image changed when a woman took charge. In

1981, Jacqueline, the 20-year-old daughter of the 'Ann Summers' owner, David Gold, attended a fashion sales party in an East London flat. Afterwards, the women asked if Jacqueline would run a similar, 'bit of a giggle' event selling her Dad's skimpy underwear and sex toys. The rest is history; the Ann Summers' Party was born.

Jacqueline Gold is a modern suffragette. She took on a male-dominated market, and now heads up an international sex 'n' suspenders empire where women can crack a whip. Any serious knicker collection has to include this label. I bought my example in Exeter; my eldest daughter waited outside the shop (there is only so much of mother's eccentricity she can take). Inside, the choice was educative. This is a long way from Jane Austen, m'dears. Lots of black lace, red fluff, and vibrating rabbits. I

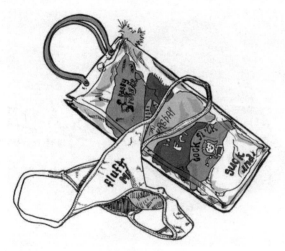

bought a pouchful of 'Monday to Sunday' themed neon thongs (G-strings now pensioners) sporting adult reading material. The shop was extremely busy but the girl on the till had time to notice and admire my Victorian cameo brooch.

'Bet she thought you a weirdo, Mother,' said my daughter when I told her, pushing my sinful thongs to the bottom of the basket.

Before I forget, I must mention a superb pair of knickers that were sent by Judith, who I met at a 'Growing Old Disgracefully' seminar. She furnished me with a fine pair of ladies' 1950s, red-woollen longjohns, with red lace on the leg-ends. They were bought at Rackhams, Birmingham, made from wool and nylon by Smedley and called 'GayJay'. I may wear them to church this winter.

I know what it is to be gripped with rampant knick-er envy.

Recently the Vicar and I went to a local amateur dramatics' production, and I fell in love with a pair of knickers used in the show. These blue knickers were knockout. Reader, I lusted for them. When the show ended, Lesley, my playwriting friend, real-ising my longing, let me have them for a modest price. They are Big Big Knickers with a spray of pink flowers embroidered on one side, made from viscose and cotton, in size 66-68 inches. The label is 'Wild Orchid', which is the largest lingerie retailer in Russia (216 stores). They opened their first UK store at Bluewater, Kent in August 2007. I read that expansion to other parts is planned. Watch this space.

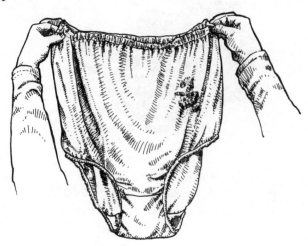

Kent makes me remember something tucked in a battered suitcase in my Costume Room. It is a bit tacky; black nylon with wobbly plastic eyes and a red bobble nose – a posing pouch left over from Comic Relief's Red Nose Day. Over the years, I have done talks for the National Trust on 'heritage' knickers, particularly in Kent, and it was one of the lovely, enthusiastic organisers, Mike, who gave me this as a present. I ♥ you, Orpington.

With global warming more than a threat, is there a pair of knickers that can make a difference? Yes.

I chanced on an advertisement for 'GreenKnickers', and, intrigued, looked up the website www.greenknickers.org. This firm does some pretty, organic, good-for-the-earth and you, Fairtrade knickers (and some guys' boxers). I bought a pair of very green, padded cycling knickers that arrived in a little green box. No, I don't ride a bicycle, but the style intrigued me, and I applaud Sarah Lucy Smith and Rose Cleary-Southwood, for bravely starting this ethical company and giving it such a quirky, eco-friendly name. Good luck to you. Check them out. The Cycling Knickers are 100 per cent, locally handmade cotton ('breathable and comfortable'), with low-impact dye and made in the UK. The pad is removable; it is Velcroed on under the knicker crotch. They are practical and saddle-proof. On the label it states; 'reduces soreness and can be removed when you reach your destination'. Or not.

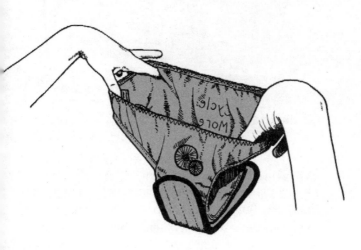

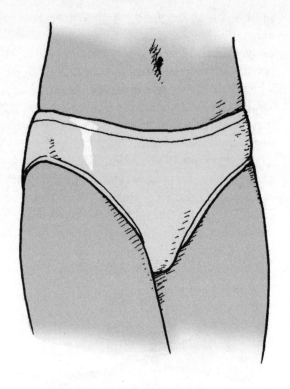

In the end, knickers appear to have lots going for them: humanity, humour, sex appeal and unending fashionability. Considering their history, after a dilly-dally start they have made up for lost time.

Doubtless, there are women who never wear knickers, but most women do, and, being fickle, will continue to want a big choice of products. Choice is the modern expectation. Our shops are crammed with knickers, they can be ordered on the Internet, and newspapers and magazines constantly persuade with the latest desirable items. The Western world loves knickers – so every shape, size, colour and occasion are catered for. Plain, fancy, sensible, sexy or kinky. They are all there. Knickers to suit every need, pocket, purse or credit card. You're buying, Madam…..Sir.

Tesco, like most supermarkets, sells knickers. Lots of them. I wandered round a Tesco in Newcastle, bemused at the sheer amount of knickery hanging from the stacks. In a way, they are all minor works of art and technology. After my usual indecision, I purchased a twinpack of 'Florence & Fred' seamfree hi-legs in nude. This pantie has the lot: comfort, well-made, smooth as a baby's bottom, slides over bumpy bits, washes and dries like a dream – and is as cheap as chips. £4 for two pairs. Girls, what more do you want? Would Mrs. Pankhurst have had it so good?

Occasionally, people ask me; 'What do you wear, Rosemary?'

'Clean ones, darling.'